THE OFFICIAL ANNUAL 2018

Written by Matt Joyce, Iain Pearce & Zoe Rundle
Designed by Chris Payne

A Grange Publication

© 2017. Published by Grange Communications Ltd., Edinburgh, under licence from AFC Bournemouth. Printed in the EU.

Photographs © Robin Jones, Amy Maidment, www.gettyimages.com

ISBN: 978-1-911287-66-7

CONTENTS

MEET
EDDIE
HOWE

LET'S KEEP EDDIE!

Two years later Eddie returned home to Dean Court on loan and he showed he was fit again and ready to play with Bournemouth.

The Cherries didn't have enough money to keep Eddie permanently – so the fans joined together to help raise the funds to bring him back for good!

The fans were right about their hero, Eddie re-joined and came close to the play-offs the next season with the Cherries. Bournemouth manager Kevin Bond saw Eddie's coaching potential and made him a player-coach, then injury struck again and Eddie had to hang up his boots aged 29.

EARLY ON, EDDIE MAKES THE GRADE

Eddie joined the Cherries when he was just 17-years-old and it didn't take him long to get started - he made his first-team debut a year later against Hull City!

An assured and commanding centre back, Eddie made over 200 appearances for the Cherries during his first spell playing at the club.

Eddie headed to Pompey in 2002 and joined up with former Bournemouth manager Harry Redknapp. However, knee injuries made his time at Fratton Park difficult and limited his appearances.

TIME TO MANAGE THE CHERRIES

December 31st 2008 was a big day for Eddie and Bournemouth. With no manager, Eddie was asked to lead the Cherries as a caretaker – and two games later he was given the job for keeps!

The club were in big trouble in League Two, but despite a 17-point penalty Eddie pulled off the Great Escape with a magnificent 2-1 win over Grimsby Town at Dean Court.

UP, UP AND AWAY!

Eddie and the Cherries didn't look back after that! In 2010 they soared to League Two promotion, even though they couldn't sign any new players that season.

In 2011 Eddie had a spell managing Burnley but soon came home to Bournemouth and in 2013 he led the Cherries to the Championship for the second time in their history.

Bournemouth finished tenth back in the Championship, not a bad start, but the next year was even better. Eddie's Cherries scored the most goals and won the league – AFC Bournemouth were in the Premier League!

Was Eddie ready for the top league? Could the Cherries stay up? Eddie's squad survived in their first Premier League season, and came an amazing ninth last season - the club's best finish ever!

THE FUTURE UNDER EDDIE

" What is next? We'll wait and see. I feel there is a lot of improvement to come. "

2017

7

VITALITY STADIUM

FACTS & FIGURES

During its early years, the stadium only had **one** small single stand!

1910

In 1910, the Cooper-Dean family donated part of their lands to the local football side, then known as Boscombe FC. The stadium built on that ground was opened the same year and received the name of Dean Court to honour the donors!

Vitality Stadium is the smallest Premier League ground and the only one seating fewer than 20,000. Only three others, Liberty Stadium, Vicarage Road and Turf Moor seat fewer than 25,000.

28,799

The record attendance at our home ground was set on 2nd March 1957, when 28,799 spectators watched an FA Cup match against Manchester United!

11,772

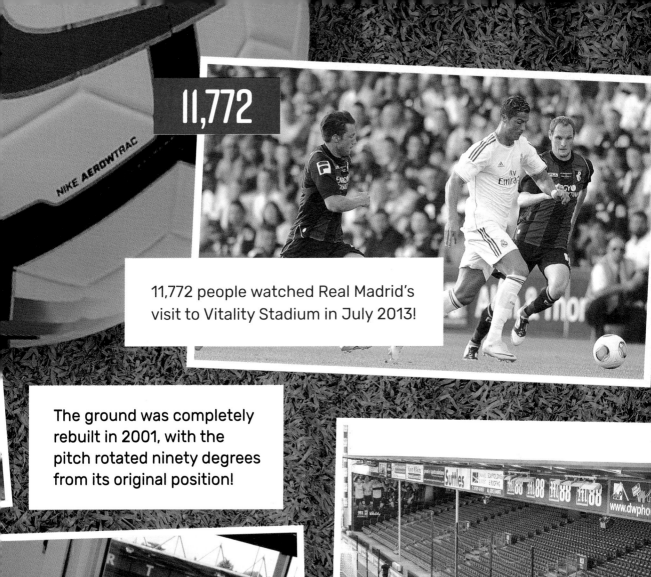

11,772 people watched Real Madrid's visit to Vitality Stadium in July 2013!

The ground was completely rebuilt in 2001, with the pitch rotated ninety degrees from its original position!

The Ted MacDougall Stand was only put up in the summer of 2013. It has a capacity of 2,400 seats and made the ground four-sided!

The Main Stand holds 14 executive boxes, a top floor restaurant, a luxury champagne lounge, press facilities, changing rooms and the tunnel!

Behind Vitality East Stand is AFC Bournemouth's wall of fame, which includes tributes to legendary Cherries players including Harry Redknapp, Luther Blissett, Jermain Defoe and George Best, as well as celebratory images of the club that go as far back as 1911!

TOP 5

HISTORIC MOMENTS

NINTH PLACE IN THE PREMIER LEAGUE

As the Cherries walked out to play Manchester United on the opening day of the 2016/17 season, no-one could predict quite how successfully Eddie Howe's side would be throughout the remainder of the campaign. Brilliant wins over Liverpool, Everton and West Ham, alongside some entertaining draws with Manchester United, Tottenham Hotspur and Arsenal, resulted in the Cherries finishing higher than ever before. Nine months after it all began, AFC Bournemouth were celebrating a top-half finish in the Premier League after a 1-1 draw with Leicester City at the King Power Stadium!

By the time the 2014/15 season began, AFC Bournemouth had only played one season in the Championship after gaining promotion from League One in 2013. Eddie Howe's side had a slow start, winning just three of their first 10 league matches. However, the boys found form at the right time and were unbeaten for 14 games between October and December. During the run-in, the Cherries were unstoppable once again, going unbeaten in their last 13 matches. A 3-0 win over Bolton at Dean Court secured AFC Bournemouth's promotion and one week later the Cherries were crowned Champions after victory against Charlton Athletic.

PROMOTED AS CHAMPIONS

2009'S GREAT ESCAPE

Before the 2008/09 season even started, the Cherries had already been docked points for financial reasons and began the campaign with a 17-point deduction. To make matters worse, not only did manager Kevin Bond leave the club in September, his replacement, Jimmy Quinn, would depart a few months later. However, up stepped Eddie Howe, who became the youngest manager in the Football League aged just 31 after taking over permanently in January. The club were still ten points away from safety at this stage and it took until the final home game of the season to secure their Football League status. Club legend Steve Fletcher scored with just ten minutes to go as the Cherries beat Grimsby 2-1.

1987 THIRD DIVISION CHAMPIONS

Champions!
Fans salute triumphant Cherries

Harry Redknapp was the man in charge for the Cherries' successful Division Three campaign in 1986/87. The side started strongly, losing just one of their opening 12 games and scoring 21 goals during that time. However, back-to-back defeats in November, including a 4-0 loss to fellow promotion rivals Middlesbrough, halted progress. More points were dropped in December, but Harry's boys would only suffer two more defeats from the turn of the year until the end of the campaign. Promotion was secured at Fulham in May, with the season finale at home to Rotherham ensuring the Cherries went up to the Second Division as champions!

1971 FOURTH DIVISION PROMOTION

The Cherries went into the 1970/71 season having just been relegated from the Third Division and with the hope of automatic promotion back up the Football League. Fred Cox's boys started extremely strongly, winning seven of their opening eight games! Their superb form continued into the new year, when the Cherries scored 19 goals in January alone. As the season drew to its close, Bournemouth and Boscombe Athletic, as the club was then known, managed to avoid defeat in nine of their last ten games, rounding off the season with a 4-0 win against York. The boys had done it and were promoted back to the Third Division on 60 points!

CHERRIES CHAPTERS

The Cherries squad has got loads of quality in our third Premier League season. It was a busy summer for the manager and the board in recruiting new faces.

We welcomed Nathan Aké and Asmir Begovic from Chelsea and Jermain Defoe came to us from Sunderland.

All three returned to the club after previous spells, while both Steve Cook and Harry Arter - both influential to our success and rise through the leagues - signed new contracts.

So, how have all five of these players got to where they are now? We'll be taking a look back at their careers to date, starting with our Premier League winning goalkeeper!

ASMIR BEGOVIC

GOALKEEPER

EARLY DAYS

Born in Bosnia, Asmir actually grew up in Canada after his family moved when he was just 10-years-old. He played Minor League Soccer in Edmonton and soon earnt a call-up to Canada's under-17 squad.

His brilliant performances saw both Spurs and Pompey show interest and the shot-stopper chose to join the Blues in 2003.

GAINING EXPERIENCE

After two years in Portsmouth's youth team, Asmir moved into the senior squad. He was immediately sent out on loan to gain some experience.

Macclesfield Town was where the Bosnian spent his first loan spell, making his Football League debut in a 1-1 draw against Stockport. Unfortunately, an injury cut his stay short and he soon returned to Portsmouth.

After recovering, Asmir was then loaned to the Cherries, making eight league appearances before being recalled. However, with England international David James brought in for Portsmouth, he was loaned out again, firstly to Yeovil and then Ipswich.

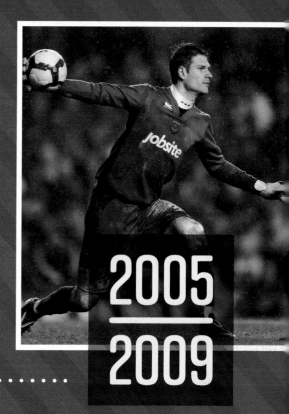

**2005
2009**

BACK TO PORTSMOUTH

November 2009 saw Asmir brought back to Portsmouth from his loan spell at Portman Road.

Upon his return to Fratton Park, the Bosnian went on to play a total of 15 times for the Blues before the season came to an end.

His brilliant performances between the sticks caught the eye of fellow Premier League outfit Stoke City and Asmir soon signed for the club in February 2010.

FIRST TEAM FOOTBALL

Asmir settled in well and made his Potters debut against Chelsea in April 2010. He soon kept his first clean sheet when Stoke faced Everton the week after.

During his first full season at the club, he was handed the number one shirt by Tony Pulis. Asmir made his first league appearance of the campaign in October and his superb performances saw him remain in the starting line-up throughout the season.

The 'keeper retained his position as Pulis' first choice 'keeper as Stoke finished 14th in the 2011/12 season. The following year, he was on top form again and conceded just 12 times in the opening 15 matches. As a result, he won the club's Player of the Year award for his efforts.

ESTABLISHED PREMIER LEAGUE 'KEEPER

With new manager Mark Hughes coming in ahead of the 2013/14 season, Asmir yet again retained his position, putting in an excellent man-of-the-match performance against Liverpool on the opening day.

His highlight of the season was undoubtedly scoring after just 13 seconds against Southampton as his long kick caught out none other than Artur Boruc!

The Bosnian's consistency showed when he was forced to miss his first league match for almost two years on Boxing Day in 2013 after breaking his finger! However, Asmir still played 33 times as the Potters went on to finish in a remarkable ninth place.

THE CHAMPIONS COME CALLING

After Stoke finished ninth for the second season in a row and Asmir kept his 50th clean sheet for the club, there was a lot of speculation surrounding his future.

It was the Champions Chelsea that won the race and the shot-stopper signed in the summer of 2015.

Asmir played regularly in his first season at Chelsea making 17 Premier League appearances.

Though mainly used as a back-up to Thibaut Courtois in his second season, Asmir did get a run in the team following a red card for the Belgian. He did superbly, keeping a sequence of clean sheets for the Blues, including one in the Champions League against Tel Aviv.

2015-2017

2017

BACK DOWN SOUTH

Still only 30-years-old and hopeful of some first-team football, the Cherries came knocking on the door wanting to secure Asmir's signature ahead of the 2017/18 Premier League campaign.

10 years after his loan spell, he returned and signed a long-term deal with the club.

WHAT IT'S LIKE TO...

SCORE YOUR FIRST PREMIER LEAGUE GOAL
BENIK AFOBE

"Of course it's up there as a career highlight. When the ball hit the net it's an unbelievable feeling that words can't describe. I've dreamt of that moment since I was a little boy and I've had to work hard to get to the top. Hopefully there's a lot more to come of course!"

CAPTAIN THE SIDE
SIMON FRANCIS

"I talk about character a lot when I speak about this group of players but it's been an honour to captain such a fearless and confident squad."

PLAY UNDER THE MANAGER
DAN GOSLING

"I feel as though I've improved massively working under the manager and the coaching staff. The ambition was always to get to the Premier League when I first joined and from day one since I saw the manager's work ethic it felt like we were a part of something good."

MAKE YOUR PREMIER LEAGUE DEBUT
BAILY CARGILL

"I was really nervous, it was against Manchester United at Old Trafford and we were having to defend. I just wanted to go on and make sure I didn't concede, my performance wasn't really in my mind. The most important thing was for us not to concede while I was on the field and coming out of the game I was happy with that."

SCORE AT A WORLD CUP
JERMAIN DEFOE

"As a young lad it's something you dream about. I was lost for words at the time and it's certainly one of the highlights of my career, to score a winning goal in a World Cup game."

MAKE YOUR DEBUT FOR YOUR COUNTRY
HARRY ARTER

"It felt like a special moment. My family didn't go over for the game but they were all watching at home. After the game I had a lot of messages from friends and family, so that was nice. It's always an honour to play for your country."

"Thankfully I got a medal and to be part of that team was great. It's a great achievement to have in your career."

WIN THE PREMIER LEAGUE
ASMIR BEGOVIC

WIN THE EUROPA LEAGUE
NATHAN AKE

"I was only 18 at the time, I played in the semi-final and to be on the bench in the final was a great experience for me. Winning the final was amazing for me and I still carry that with me. The fact it was in Holland meant a lot of people I know were able to come and watch so that made it even more special."

SCORE A PREMIER LEAGUE HAT-TRICK
CALLUM WILSON

"Any goal in the Premier League is massive but on a personal note it made my confidence go sky high. It was a good time to score it too because it showed we can score in the Premier League and make our mark. I look back on that moment with great pride."

RISE THROUGH THE LEAGUES
MARC PUGH

"Lots of players have started off in the Premier League and had it handed to them on a plate but we've had to work our way up the ladder. But what a journey this club has been on, it's been a pleasure to be a part of and one that might not get repeated again."

BRIGHTON DAYS

Born in Sussex, Steve is a product of the Brighton and Hove Albion academy and was only 17-years-old when he made his first team debut for the club in a League Cup win over Manchester City.

Soon impressing, the defender was selected for the league game against Crewe Alexandra early the following year and went on to sign his first professional contract at the end of the season.

LOAN AFTER LOAN

In November 2009, almost a year after a brief loan spell with Havant & Waterlooville, Steve was sent on loan to Conference South side Eastleigh on the lookout for some experience.

He played ten league games for the Spitfires before returning to Brighton – ready to be loaned out to Eastbourne Borough.

Steve settled well at Priory Lane and scored one goal in seven appearances. He was so good Eastbourne wanted to extend his loan, however Mansfield was the next temporary destination for the defender.

2011 - 2012

CHERRIES COME CALLING

Steve's performances attracted attention from Bournemouth in League One. After eight strong loan appearances in 2011, the January transfer window soon opened and the Cherries wanted to keep him.

In fact, Steve's performances on loan had been so amazing that Eddie Howe signed him for keeps on a three-and-a-half year deal!

CHERRIES CHAPTER

STEVE COOK

DEFENDER

COOKIE PLAYS MAJOR ROLE IN PROMOTIONS

The following season saw Steve keep his place in the starting line-up and he made 29 appearances for the Cherries.

In the team and soon in the Championship! Steve's 38 appearances in 2012/13 saw the side promoted to the Championship after finishing second in League One.

After a season settling into the second tier, it didn't take long for the Cherries to climb again! Steve played every game as Eddie Howe's boys were promoted to the Premier League for the first time. He also scored a total of five goals across the campaign, including strikes in the brilliant 5-1 win at Fulham and an excellent 4-2 victory over Birmingham.

PREMIER LEAGUE HERO

As the Cherries walked out against Aston Villa in their first ever Premier League match, Steve's performances for the club ensured his place in the starting XI and Bournemouth history.

He had his shooting boots on once again, as he netted four Premier League goals that season and in 2016/17 Steve really made his mark and had his best campaign to date.

He was one of just three outfield players to play every single minute of the Premier League season and even won the Bournemouth Echo's Player of the Season award.

Steve's strike against Liverpool, in the brilliant 4-3 win, also saw him pick up the top goal at the end of season awards night.

TOP 5

VITALITY STADIUM PREMIER LEAGUE MOMENTS

AFC BOURNEMOUTH
SUNDERLAND

2
0

Matt Ritchie lit up Vitality Stadium as we grabbed our first ever home Premier League win! Callum Wilson span round the Black Cats' defence to power home after only four minutes... and then Matt raised the roof with a second. In came a Cherries corner and as it flew to the edge of the box there was Matt to chest and blast home an unstoppable volley!

AFC BOURNEMOUTH 2
MANCHESTER UNITED 1

We got our first win against the Red Devils in over 30 years and Junior Stanislas scored from a corner after only 100 seconds! Marouane Fellaini made it 1-1 but there was no stopping the Cherries, and it was even a former United player who won us the game. Joshua King swept home a shot from a corner as he sent Vitality Stadium wild and showed his old team what they were missing!

AFC BOURNEMOUTH 2
SOUTHAMPTON 0

There was only one team on the south coast after this win! First Steve Cook acrobatically volleyed home before Benik Afobe made himself an instant Vitality hero with the second. Benik had only been with us a few weeks but scored his second home goal to give the Cherries fans an evening to remember!

AFC BOURNEMOUTH 6
HULL CITY 1

We hit Hull City for six in the biggest Premier League win yet for the Cherries! Charlie Daniels gave us the lead, but soon Hull were level. No worries though, five more goals followed as the team ran riot, as Junior Stanislas scored two, Steve Cook, Callum Wilson and Dan Gosling all added their name to the tally to secure the club's first ever Premier League six goal haul! Stanislas had one of his best games for the club as not only did he score two, he made two goals as well!

AFC BOURNEMOUTH 4
LIVERPOOL 3

What a game – and one of the Premier League's best ever comebacks! The Cherries were 2-0 down thanks to goals from Sadio Mane and Divock Origi when Ryan Fraser came on and changed everything. Wee Man won us a penalty, scored and soon it was 3-3 with just minutes left...in came a shot and Nathan Ake was there to bundle home a sensational rebound!

25

MY FIRST...

SWAPPED SHIRT

My first swapped shirt would've been with Cesc Fabregas with Chelsea, it was our first year in the Premier League and we were beaten 4-1 but he said he respected the way we play out from the back and our style of football.

FA CUP GOAL

It was in League Two with Bury. I was 19 and we played in the FA Cup against Weymouth on TV and I scored a tap in.

WITH
MARC PUGH

CLUB PLAYED FOR

I played for my local team called Waterfoot. We played really high up on a hill called the Glen and the wind at the games was horrendous. It was downhill as well so I used to nick a few goals from the halfway line!

SQUAD NUMBER

As long as I've known, I've always been 7. It's my favourite number – I've had it for ten years now.

FOOTBALL HERO

There was two. I was a real admirer of Giggs and Cantona. Cantona just because he was an absolute legend and Giggs because he played in a similar position to me. I went to Carrington once or twice when I was young and got a photo with Cantona. Great memories!

CAR

My first car was a Renault Clio which my mum and dad bought for me on my 18th birthday. After a while I had to climb in the passenger seat side because the driver's door wouldn't open, all part and parcel of your first car.

PAIR OF BOOTS

My first pair of boots were Puma Kings. I used to pepper them with dubbin to make them look brand new - I did that for about four or five years 'til my feet grew out of them.

PROFESSIONAL CLUB GAME

I went on loan to the Conference from Burnley when I was 17 and we played Lincoln City away. I scored on my debut actually - so it was a memorable one.

MANAGER

My professional manager was Chris Casper who signed me with Bury. We had a really good relationship - until I rejected a contract and then he went a bit sour!

HARRY ARTER

MIDFIELDER

STARTING OUT

Born in Sidcup, Harry began his career at Charlton Athletic and was a prominent member of their youth teams until 2007.

It was in September that year that the Republic of Ireland international made his professional debut for the club, coming off the bench in the 86th minute of the Addicks' League Cup tie with Luton.

2008 / 2009

HUNT FOR FIRST TEAM FOOTBALL

After failing to turn out in the league and make any further appearances for Charlton in the 2007/08 season, Arter went on loan in the hope of gaining some first-team action.

During the early months of the campaign, the then 18-year-old spent time at Staines Town, where he made four league appearances for the club in a year that saw them promoted to the Conference South.

As the season continued and drew nearer to its conclusion, Harry moved on loan to Welling United and made three league appearances for the side before returning to the Valley.

A MOVE AWAY

Unfortunately for the midfielder, Charlton released him at the end of the season and he was temporarily without a club.

Nevertheless, Arter never gave up and by June had earnt himself a contract with another Conference South side, Woking. His 36 league appearances and five goals from the centre of midfield helped the Cardinals to the play-offs, where they narrowly lost to Bath and failed to gain promotion.

It soon became apparent that Arter was playing well below his level, with a number of Football League clubs rumoured to be after his signature.

2009

SETTLING DOWN SOUTH

In June 2010, Harry was snapped up by Eddie Howe and became a Cherries player. Then in League One, he found starts hard to come by, resulting in a one-month loan to Carlisle United.

However, the following year was when Arter really established himself down south, getting off to a flying start by scoring his first goal for the club against Sheffield Wednesday in August.

That year, he continued to cement his place in the Cherries starting line-up, playing 34 times in their league campaign and scoring five goals in the process.

RISING UP THE RANKS

This season would be a pivotal one for Bournemouth's number eight. Upon Eddie Howe's return to Vitality Stadium, Arter scored twice to mark his first game back in charge, securing a 3-1 win over Tranmere Rovers.

Another of his eight goals that season also came in a 3-1 win, this time against Carlisle United in what was the penultimate game of the campaign.

The three points were enough to secure Bournemouth promotion to the Championship and it finally looked like Harry would get his chance at that level after all.

2014
2015

PREMIER LEAGUE CALLING

After a stable first season in the Championship, Arter would have a huge influence in the 2014/15 campaign, one which would go down in the history books for AFC Bournemouth.

He played his part in some impressive results, including an 8-0 win against Birmingham at St. Andrews, before coming up with some crucial goals against fellow promotion rivals Middlesbrough and Watford.

The Supporters' Player of the Season was then involved in the 3-0 home victory over Bolton which sealed promotion to the Premier League. Five days later, Arter would score against former club Charlton in another 3-0 win, which secured the Championship title for the Cherries.

PREMIER LEAGUE REGULAR

Arter was now a Premier League player and would make quite the impact in the Cherries' first season in English football's top flight.

Despite groin problems at the start of the season initially halting his progress, Harry came straight back into Eddie's side in November. The now 27-year-old scored his only goal of the season in a 3-1 loss to West Ham at Vitality stadium and also started in the wins over Southampton, Chelsea and an emotional affair with Manchester United.

As a result of his form, Arter earned himself a place on the plane for Ireland's Euro 2016 campaign where they made it through their group and narrowly lost in the Round of 16 to eventual finalists and hosts France. Unfortunately for the midfielder, he missed out on the tournament due to injury.

Last season with his injuries behind him, Arter was a regular in the Cherries midfield and put in some excellent displays against some of the world's finest talents.

TOP 5

CHERRIES LEGENDS

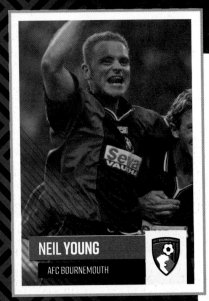

NEIL YOUNG

AFC BOURNEMOUTH

Neil Young played 507 times for the Cherries across a 14-year period. After signing from Tottenham in 1994, he made his debut later that year aged just 18.

Often deployed as a right-back, Young was also comfortable in the heart of defence and even popped up with the odd goal across his career, the first of which came in a 4-0 thrashing of Gillingham on Boxing Day in 1997.

His services to the club were rightfully awarded by a testimonial in 2005, where he fittingly played against his brother Luke's Charlton Athletic side.

Upon leaving the club in 2008, Young had made over 30 appearances in 10 of his 14 seasons with the Cherries, representing the club in both Division Two and Division Three, which later became known as League One and League Two respectively.

Sean O'Driscoll signed for AFC Bournemouth after leaving Fulham in 1984 and would go on to make 423 league appearances for the Cherries.

The midfielder managed 19 goals across his 11 years at the club, which saw him play in both Division Two and Division Three.

O'Driscoll enjoyed his most prominent season in a Cherries shirt during 1986/87 as he was part of the side which gained promotion to Division Two, winning the league and going up as Champions.

After retiring in 1995 and playing his last season in a red and black shirt, O'Driscoll returned to the club five years later to take up the vacant managerial position.

Despite a lack of funds and a few seasons hampered by injuries, the former Republic of Ireland international guided the Cherries to promotion from Division Three in 2003, before leaving for Doncaster in 2006.

SEAN O'DRISCOLL

AFC BOURNEMOUTH

MACDOUGALL
OURNEMOUTH

Ted MacDougall arrived down south in 1969 and was brought in by then manager Freddie Cox. The striker made quite the impression, netting 21 times in the league during his opening season in a Cherries shirt.

The following year, MacDougall started brightly once again, having 16 goals to his name by October, whilst he later went on to score six in one match as the Cherries comfortably overcame Oxford.

He finished the season with 42 league goals, helping the side gain promotion back to Division Three. But, the striker wasn't done yet.

As the 1971/72 campaign got underway, MacDougall had soon netted nine goals in a single game as the side beat Margate 11-0 in the FA Cup. Finishing the season on no less than 35 league goals, he was a much wanted man.

Despite leaving that summer, MacDougall would return to the club six years later and he hadn't lost his finishing touch. His two seasons back in a Cherries shirt saw him manage 16 goals in 52 league appearances, whilst his contributions across the two spells were rewarded with a stand named after him in July 2013.

Fletcher first featured in an AFC Bournemouth shirt in 1992, with his first stint at the club lasting 15 years. In total, he made 781 appearances and netted 121 goals for the Cherries as well as gaining promotion to Division Two via the play-offs in 2003.

After leaving in 2007, Fletcher returned two years later with more success coming his way. Within the striker's first season back, he helped the Cherries to a second-placed finish in League Two and consequently promotion to League One.

The following year, Fletcher was part of the squad that finished in the League One play-off places but narrowly missed out on promotion. However, it only took a year to make amends and, in his last season playing professional football, he helped the Cherries finish second and secure Championship football.

Nowadays, 'Fletch' remains with the Cherries as a first-team coach, working alongside former teammates Eddie Howe and Jason Tindall, and still holds the club record for the most league appearances with 514.

STEVE FLETCHER
AFC BOURNEMOUTH

DIE HOWE
AFC BOURNEMOUTH

The Cherries manager started his affiliation with AFC Bournemouth in 1994, making his debut as an 18-year-old. His initial spell at the Cherries lasted eight years, where he made 237 appearances in a Cherries shirt. During that time, Howe helped the side remain in Division Two and even bagged 13 goals from the heart of defence.

After two years at Portsmouth and a brief spell at Swindon, he returned to Bournemouth after fans came together to help fund his transfer. However, despite remaining with the Cherries for three years, the former England under-21 international was hampered by injuries and only made a total of 57 appearances in all competitions, subsequently being forced into retirement

Of course, we all know what he's done for us as a manager, simply unbelievable!

ADVICE FROM THE PROS

RETURNING FROM INJURY
TYRONE MINGS

"Don't rush it, especially with a serious injury it's easy to get upset and lose focus of what you want to achieve. As long as you can come back fitter and stronger and you don't lose your love for the game then that'll see you through."

CALMING YOUR NERVES BEFORE A BIG GAME
ASMIR BEGOVIC

"Try and keep things as normal as possible. Be it a game in the World Cup or any other big game it's important to keep the same routine. Don't change your preparations even if you're feeling nervous and you'll become more comfortable."

EING READY TO GO ON AS A SUBSTITUTE
BAILY CARGILL

You need to be mentally ready, you have to prepare as though you're going to be playing, even if you're on the bench. The most important thing is that you're ready to go at any time.

"

SETTLING INTO NEW SURROUNDINGS
EMERSON HYNDMAN

"
The key is to be yourself and relate to your new team-mates as much as you can. At the same time you need to stay who you are. The biggest thing for me moving from the USA was the culture change and as soon as I adjusted to that I was set to go.
"

IMPROVING YOUR FINISHING
JERMAIN DEFOE

"
Practise, practise, practise! Do it all day, I used to stay behind at training and practise with both feet. I speak to a lot of kids and they say they practise, I ask them if they use both feet and they say no. Take the time to practise and you'll get better.
"

JOSHUA KING

FORWARD

CHERRIES CHA

MOVE TO ENGLAND

2008

Born in Oslo in Norway, Joshua began his career with his local club Rosmas, where he regularly played with the older age ranges at the club.

When he was 15, he moved to Valerenga, another Norwegian club, before playing in the Nike Premier Cup at Old Trafford. After that, Joshua trained with Manchester United on several occasions.

UEFA rules meant that the striker couldn't sign for the Red Devils until he was 16 but he rejected Chelsea to join the Reds in 2008!

START TO LIFE AS A RED

King quickly impressed at Old Trafford and made his under-18s debut against Sunderland in March 2008.

He continued to learn under Warren Joyce at United's Academy and he started the 2008/09 season on fire, scoring four goals in four matches as the Manchester United Under-17s won the 2008 Milk Cup.

After that, an injury meant King would miss three months before returning in January to make his Reserve Team debut.

THE BREAKTHROUGH

Joshua's impressive form for the reserves meant that Sir Alex Ferguson was keen to give the young striker an opportunity in the first team. He came on as a substitute for his Reds debut, coming on in the EFL Cup for his good friend Danny Welbeck in September 2009.

This provoked League One side Preston North End to sign Joshua on loan and give him regular first team football: he made ten appearances and scored once during his loan at Deepdale. After his return to Manchester United, King was a regular in the Reserves, playing in 17 of the last 18 games of the season.

MORE FIRST TEAM FOOTBALL

2010

Joshua would again spend the 2010/11 season away from Old Trafford in two loan spells, the first of which was with German side Borussia Monchengladbach.

He started well at Gladbach but a groin injury halted his progress in the Bundesliga, meaning he returned to England after two substitute appearances. During his time in Germany though, Joshua made his international debut at just the age of 19.

Another move from Old Trafford followed with Hull City, who he joined in January 2012. Joshua played 18 times for the Tigers in the Championship as his reputation continued to grow.

2011

MOVE AWAY

Joshua started the 2012/13 season strongly for United, making his Champions League debut for the club against Galatasaray in the group stage. But as an ambitious player, Joshua wanted first-team football to make him develop and he moved permanently away from Old Trafford to Blackburn Rovers.

There was plenty of competition for places at Ewood Park as Jordan Rhodes, Nuno Gomes and Colin Kazim-Richards were all at the club, but King proved his own and earned his spot in the team.

MORE ROVERS SUCCESS

King played out wide a lot during his time with Rovers, but was a constant menace to the opposition.

He made 66 appearances for the club and arguably his highlight, was scoring a memorable FA Cup hat-trick against Premier League side Stoke City when Rovers were 4-1 winners at Ewood Park.

That happened in the 2014/15 season where he scored six goals in total which alerted one club in particular...

A PREMIER MOVE DOWN SOUTH

Upon the Cherries' promotion to the top flight, Eddie Howe made Joshua his third signing of the summer for an undisclosed fee.

King had returned to the Premier League and told afcb.co.uk when he signed: "The Premier League has always been the dream to play in. I've seen what the manager has done with the squad here and the football Bournemouth play suits me very well I think."

A MOMENT TO REMEMBER

Joshua adapted to life back in the Premier League with ease, but there was one moment that stood out above all others.

The Cherries were in a deadlock against Manchester United, Joshua's former team. Junior Stanislas' corner had flown into the net before Marouane Fellaini equalised for the visitors.

But the team that brought the striker to England were made to pay, as he scored the winner against them to give the club not only a hard-fought win against world class opposition, but one of the biggest wins in the club's history.

The Norwegian went on to score six more goals as the Cherries survived in the Premier League at the first time of asking!

2015/16

2016-2017

A PREMIER LEAGUE LEADER

Last season was a memorable one for King, who was one of the form strikers in the entire country in 2017. He scored three goals in the first half of the season, before he went on an unbelievable scoring streak – netting 13 times in 16 games.

Not only did Joshua bag his goals against ten different clubs, but his tally included a memorable hat-trick against West Ham United. On top of that, the striker's goals directly led the Cherries to gaining 12 points, only Sergio Aguero or Diego Costa could point to more in the league!

TOP 5
PREMIER LEAGUE AWAY DAYS

CHELSEA | 7 DECEMBER 2015

1

Possibly the most memorable result in the club's history, the Cherries were 1-0 winners over the then-reigning Premier League champions Chelsea away from home. But it was no fluke, the Cherries played extremely well and Glenn Murray scored as the Blues failed to clear a corner late on.

Murray had only been on the field for 99 seconds before heading in the famous goal at Stamford Bridge, with the strike making the club the first promoted side to beat Chelsea at home since Charlton in April 2001!

2. WEST HAM UNITED

A seven goal thriller and of course, a first ever Premier League for AFC Bournemouth came at Upton Park in 2015.

Callum Wilson stole the show with a magical hat-trick, while Marc Pugh added a strike in a topsy-turvy clash in the capital. Wilson netted twice before Mark Noble scored a penalty for West Ham and Cheikhou Kouyate levelled.

Pugh then curled in a sublime strike before Wilson notched a penalty – with Modibo Maiga netting late on.

But the Cherries secured a huge Premier League victory, with Wilson becoming only the fifth player in Premier League history to score an away hat-trick for a newly promoted side.

3. NEWCASTLE

A long trip north, the Cherries went into their clash at St. James' Park having just beat rivals Southampton at Vitality Stadium.

The crowd was extremely hostile as the Toon Army were fighting relegation, but the Cherries got off to a great start and Steven Taylor diverted into his own net to open the scoring.

In the second half, Joshua King slammed in before Ayoze Perez made it a nervy finish. But Charlie Daniels' wonderful drilled strike gave the Cherries another memorable Premier League win up north.

4. LIVERPOOL

Many teams have been overpowered over the years at Anfield, but last season, the Cherries proved they were no pushovers by securing a point against the Reds.

Benik Afobe latched onto a back pass to score the opener, before Phillipe Coutinho equalised for the Reds.

The home side turned up the pressure and went ahead through Divock Origi but Joshua King's late strike, an instinctive finish in the area, secured a memorable point for the Cherries at one of the most unique stadiums in world football.

5. SUNDERLAND

With the Cherries looking to avoid relegation last season, a long trip to Sunderland could all but secure the club's status for another top-flight season.

It was a tight, scrappy affair, with Sunderland throwing everything at the defence as they needed to win to stop themselves from being relegated.

But Lys Mousset found Ryan Fraser who drove down the right-hand side and picked out Joshua King in the middle who continued his scoring run to give the Cherries a huge three points and pretty much meant that the 2017/18 season would be one in the Premier League!

CLUB PLAYED FOR

Eclipse – a team in Essex, in Chadwell Heath when I was six-years-old. They've folded now though!

FOOTBALL HERO

Theirry Henry and the Brazilian Ronaldo. I count them both equally, I always looked up to them and tried to copy their game – they could be the best strikers ever.

PAIR OF BOOTS

Red pumas. A pair of red puma kings when I was six years old.

PROFESSIONAL GOAL

I was 17 and it was while I was at Huddersfield. It was an away game at Rotherham and I scored twice that day. It was a decent goal, we won 5-2!

PROFESSIONAL CLUB GAME

My first club game was Huddersfield vs Sheffield Wednesday when I was on loan when I was 17. That was back in 2011 and I thought I played quite well. We won 2-0, I didn't score but I enjoyed it.

SQUAD NUMBER

Number 24. I much prefer having number nine now!

MY FIRST...

SWAPPED SHIRT

I'm having to go back far now... My first swapped shirt was with Gerard Deulofeu – who's at Barcelona now - in an England under 17s game against Spain.

HAT-TRICK

That came when I was on loan at MK Dons. It was against Colchester and we were in great form at the time and we won 6-0.

MANAGER

My first manager professionally was Lee Clarke at Huddersfield, I enjoyed working with him and he was a great manager for me.

WITH BENIK AFOBE

EARLY DAYS

Jermain was born in London and started his professional career at West Ham. At just 18-years-old, he was sent on loan to the Cherries to gain some experience and he was brilliant!

12 goals in 10 consecutive games saw him tipped for a big future and he could return to West Ham full of confidence.

Jermain enjoyed two years in the first team at Upton Park. He scored 14 goals in the 2001/02 season and finished as top scorer, before netting a further 11 the year after. However, it wasn't enough to keep the Hammers up and he was soon on the move.

1994-2004

2004
2008

MOVE TO NORTH LONDON

Jermain's next club was Spurs and he signed in 2004. His first full season with the club saw him score a fantastic 13 goals, including a hat-trick against Southampton. The striker also managed to net nine times in only eight cup games.

In the following two years, the England international was used in rotation with fellow forward Robbie Keane, but he still competed in the UEFA Cup for the first time and even reached 50 goals for Spurs.

After four years, Jermain wanted more first-team football and his excellent goal-scoring reputation earnt himself a move to Pompey after a brief spell on loan.

JERMAIN DEFOE

FORWARD

2008

A YEAR DOWN SOUTH

Jermain made a superb start to life down south, netting in his first five games at Fratton Park and becoming the first ever Pompey player to do so.

He was unfortunately cup-tied for the club's FA Cup success, but did remain a crucial part of the side ahead of the 2008/09 season. His biggest contribution came after scoring and assisting in Portsmouth's first ever game in Europe as they beat Portuguese side Vitoria de Guimaraes 2-0.

RETURN TO SPURS

2014

Harry Redknapp's departure at Portsmouth saw Jermain follow him back to Spurs as the striker began his second spell at the club.

His first full season back in North London saw him finish on 24 goals for the year, after an excellent hat-trick against Hull and five terrific goals he netted against Wigan in a 9-1 win. Towards the end of the season, Defoe's goals against Chelsea and Arsenal sealed famous victories.

In the next three years, Jermain managed to score between 10 and 20 goals each season for Spurs. He also made his Champions League debut and reached 100 goals both for Tottenham and in the Premier League!

However, as the 2013/14 campaign got underway, Jermain found starts hard to come by and went abroad for the first time in his career.

A MOVE AWAY

Jermain signed for Toronto in early 2014 and made his debut on the first day of the MLS season. He made an immediate impact, netting both goals in a 2-1 victory over Seattle Sounders.

The striker continued to find the target and managed 11 goals in 19 league appearances and soon attracted Premier League attention once again.

PREMIER LEAGUE RETURN

Jermain signed for the Black Cats in January 2015, with his most notable contribution that year coming in the Tyne-Wear derby. He scored a brilliant 22-yard volley to secure Sunderland a famous win and help the side remain in the Premier League for another year.

The following year saw Jermain help the Black Cats narrowly avoid the drop once again. Two goals against fellow strugglers Villa and a tremendous hat-trick against Swansea helped remove Sunderland from the drop zone. They later secured safety thanks to Jermain's goal on the final day of the season against Premier League giants Chelsea.

However, the striker's 15 goals in the 2016/17 campaign couldn't help Sunderland stay up, but he did manage to get back in the England team, as well as net his 150th top flight goal in November!

2015
2017

STILL GOING STRONG

Upon Sunderland's relegation, AFC Bournemouth were keen to snap up Jermain. It was then announced in June that the striker had signed a three-year-deal with the club and would return 16 years on from his loan spell.

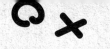

ADVICE FROM THE PROS

STEPPING UP A LEVEL AS A STRIKER
BENIK AFOBE

"Always believe in yourself, even if you miss the easy ones and people are laughing just keep going because eventually practise makes perfect and you're going to start hitting the back of the net sooner or later. Also make sure you are enjoying it – never put too much pressure on yourself."

HOW TO BE A GOOD CAPTAIN
SIMON FRANCIS

"You've got to lead by example, that's the main thing. People around you will take your lead on things and act how you act. As a captain you've got to act in the right manner at all times because you're not just representing yourself, you're representing the team as well. If you act well hopefully others will follow."

IMPRESSING A NEW MANAGER
NATHAN AKÉ

"First and foremost you have to show that you want to play. Always give 100%, that's a must, and outside of training try to do the extras, show the manager in as many ways as possible that you want to play and make sure you're ready to play if you get the call."

DEALING WITH A NEW INJURY
JUNIOR STANISLAS

"If you're injured then keep the right people around you, positive people, and stay away from any negativity. You need to try and keep your mind fresh, if you're not playing you need to work hard and keep doing the things you can do to get back fit and into the team."

PROVING YOU DESERVE A STARTING SPOT IN THE TEAM
MARC PUGH

"You've got to show belief and work hard day-in day-out. I've seen a lot of players who have talent but haven't had the dedication and work rate. The will to succeed beats talent any day."

TOP 5
HAT-TRICK HEROES

CALLUM WILSON
v WEST HAM UNITED

Callum's hat-trick at West Ham United in our first Premier League season set all kinds of records!

The striker showed his deadly form to help us to a 4-3 win, which was our first ever Premier League victory. It was Callum's first professional treble and his first strike, a cool first time finish from Simon Francis' cross, was our first ever top flight goal!

It's Wilson's only hat-trick for the club so far and it was an unforgettable day in our last ever game at Upton Park.

STEVE FLETCHER
v BRENTFORD

Legendary striker Fletcher had spent 13 seasons on the south coast before he scored his first ever career hat-trick!

After 480 appearances and scoring twice in a game on nine occasions, Fletch finally bagged three goals against Brentford in a 3-2 win on New Year's Day in 2005.

The big man said of his hat-trick: "I've scored a few 'double-baggers' in my time, but I can't even remember scoring a hat-trick in training.

"I've had a bit of banter with supporters about how I was never going to get one, but it's finally come 15 years into my career!"

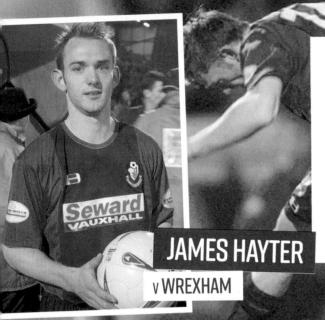

14 years have passed since former Cherries frontman Hayter shocked the entire football world.

One of the most famous trebles of all time, not just for us but in Football League history, Hayter took to the field on 85 minutes with the Cherries already 3-0 up against Wrexham.

Unbelievably, 140-seconds later, Hayter had scored three times and the team went 6-0 up!

It remains the quickest ever Football League hat-trick and it was so fast, that his mum and dad who travelled to watch him missed all the goals!

JAMES HAYTER
v WREXHAM

v DONCASTER ROVERS
JANN KERMORGANT

Former striker Yann Kermorgant signed in January 2014 and had been used as a sub in his first four games until his first start in March. What followed was a dream for big Yann, who scored a hat-trick on his first home start for the club against Doncaster Rovers.

He scored a lovely volley to get his first, before he headed in from two Simon Francis crosses to secure an eye-catching moment. That started a memorable Cherries career for Kermorgant who scored 27 times in total for the club, this was his only hat-trick though!

In February 2007, Darren Anderton netted the only hat-trick of his 18-year career!

The former Tottenham Hotspur hero, who played for England 30 times, waited 542 league games before his first treble helped the Cherries romp to a 5-0 victory at home to Leyton Orient.

His first goal came after a wonderful turn and finish just inside the box. His second was a powerful left-footed effort and his third was a tap in after good work from Steve Fletcher.

"I always thought scoring a goal was a bonus, but to get three was simply brilliant," the midfielder said.

DARREN ANDERTON
v LEYTON ORIENT

51

UMBRO GALLERY

FROM IDEA TO PRODUCT

How did we start off with an idea from Umbro and make it into the kit?

We went behind-the-scenes to see just how we got our three kits from Umbro and what went on in the process!

STEP 1

Eddie Howe and Jason Tindall like having an input into the kits, something which is unique for most Premier League clubs.

Eddie and JT met with Umbro representatives to get a feel for what they would be designing for us.

STEP 2

We officially unveiled our partnership with Umbro with a massive sand sculpture inside Vitality Stadium! Lovely stuff!

STEP 3

Vice captain Andrew Surman went to Umbro's HQ in Manchester to meet the designers and see the kit prototypes for himself.

He was impressed with what he saw! "It was great to go behind-the-scenes and see how much effort goes into the production and thought process behind the kit. Us as players, we just wear it, but seeing this shows the hard work that has been put it. It's also a great kit!"

STEP 4

The finished launch was announced on 21st June 2017, our first Umbro home kit of our new partnership!

The away and third kits have followed too: It's safe to say that win, lose or draw, the Cherries will be playing in the Premier League in some serious style!

STEVE COOK TOP 5 GOALS

ACROBATIC VOLLEY AGAINST SAINTS
SOUTHAMPTON - 1 MAR 2016

> I think everyone knows what beating Southampton means to the fans so to get the opening goal was unbelievable and I think the celebrations showed that.

STUNNING OVERHEAD KICK AT PORTMAN ROAD

> It came off the back of a poor header from myself but I picked up the flight. I got a bit lucky that it went in but it was pleasing because the Friday before we played Sheffield Wednesday and I made a mistake. It had led to a goal so it was quite nice to make up for it that way.

IPSWICH - 21 APR 2014

"The game was incredible, to come back the way we did. Obviously I got the equaliser and we felt we could go on and win it. Thankfully we did because it probably made my goal look better with the win. To score against Liverpool in such an unbelievable game was incredible."

GOAL OF THE SEASON AGAINST THE REDS

LIVERPOOL - 4 DEC 2017

UNBELIEVABLE TOP CORNER STRIKE

FULHAM - 6 MAR 2015

"This was a great night for the club. One of the best games I've experienced since I've been here. The goal was really special. Some people saw it was a cross but it was a cross-shot and it turned out to be probably the best goal that I've scored. It was a really great night."

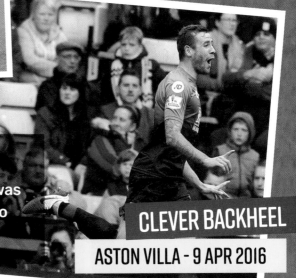

"We'd worked on it in the week and everything went to plan. It was lucky I was in the right place at the right time but to score that sort of goal was nice."

CLEVER BACKHEEL

ASTON VILLA - 9 APR 2016

MY FIRST...

PAIR OF BOOTS

They were Predators when I was really young. I had my name on them and was buzzing to be fair, might have been around 2003.

CLUB PLAYED FOR

I first played for a club when I was really young but then I joined Tadcaster Magnets where I lived in Yorkshire. I played as a 'Keeper... I hated it! I didn't like football but then I played outfield and then really enjoyed it.

WITH
LEWIS COOK

SWAPPED SHIRT

Will Hughes at Derby I think, or Demarai Gray I'm not so sure. I think it was Will Hughes', I got it signed so I didn't get it washed and I had to let it air out because it stunk! I want to put my shirts in frames.

FOOTBALL HERO

Paul Scholes. I'd watch any football and as a young kid he was the best player.

PROFESSIONAL CLUB GAME

It was for Leeds at Millwall away. I gave away a penalty and we lost 2-0, so it wasn't the best! I'm adamant the guy dived...

CAR

I shared my mum's Corsa at 17 and passed first time!

PROFESSIONAL GOAL

It was against Doncaster and I got sent off after that. I scored in the first 20 minutes then got sent off ten minutes later, this first goal and first game aren't looking good! Plenty of learning curves early on.

INTERNATIONAL

I can't remember what age I was, maybe 14 or 15, but it was the Victory Shield against Ireland. I haven't played at Wembley yet for my country so that's the goal.

MANAGER

David Hockaday gave me my debut and was there for a while, I'm thankful to him for trusting me.

SQUAD NUMBER

23, I like that number, it's my first one so I remember it. But any number is a number isn't it! 16 isn't too bad now!

QUIZ TIME

WHO AM I?

I joined the club back in 2014. I've played for clubs like Newcastle and Plymouth over my career!

I play centre midfield and scored twice last season!

WORDSEARCH

Hidden in the wordsearch below are the names of 18 AFC Bournemouth players, can you find them all? Words go horizontally, vertically, diagonally and backwards.

```
G S I C N A R F E S G N I M
E A R T E R S L E I N A D P
E B A L E B D A K E B A N U
L B O U A L E D A R G M L G
F K A F N O S L I W H A W H
O H W U A E N I H B G H O L
G W B E G O V I C R A O M E
E S U R M A N R L A D N I W
O G D E C U R O B D T E M I
D R A M S D A L E S I Y E S
D G D A H T I M S M A D A C
E N E B I M A S G I N R N O
M M G O S L I N G T I T B O
N O I E O F E D A H G C H K
```

- AKE
- BORUC
- AFOBE
- PUGH
- MAHONEY
- ADAMSMITH
- BRADSMITH
- BEGOVIC
- LEWISCOOK
- FRANCIS
- SURMAN
- ARTER
- RAMSDALE
- GOSLING
- MINGS
- IBE
- WILSON
- DEFOE

SHIRTS FROM HISTORY

 A
 B
 C
 D
 E

What year did AFC Bournemouth have the following shirts?

1999/00............. 2004/06............. 2006/08............. 2014/15............. 2015/16.............

MASSIVE MUDDLE

Can you guess these players' names – they've been muddled up!

ASMO BRICE VIG

....

CONAH ERNY MOON

....

DACHIA NIELS ERL

....

ENG MIN STORY

....

FREEMAN JODIE

....

SQUAD NUMBER CONUNDRUM

Work out these squad number numeracy questions... your answer is the player who wears that number!

1. Marc Pugh's squad number + Ryan Fraser's squad number - Junior Stanislas' squad number

= ....

2. Lys Mousset's squad number + Jordon Ibe's squad number ÷ Simon Francis' squad number - Andrew Surman's squad number

= ....

3. Steve Cook's squad number x Harry Arter's squad number - Charlie Daniels' squad number

= ....

4. Dan Golsing's squad number + Nathan Ake's squad number + Brad Smith's squad number + Artur Boruc's squad number

= ....

NAUGHTY BOY!

Which Cherries midfielder received the most yellow cards in the entire 2016/17 season?

....

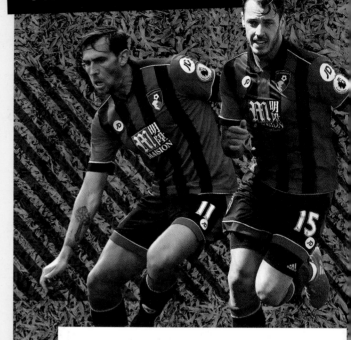

Who got more assists in the 2016/17 season - Charlie Daniels or Adam Smith?

....

NAME THE SIDE

Can you name all the players in this team photo?

1..   2..   3..

4..   5..   6..

7..

FIVE QUESTIONS ON...

1. Who was the Cherries' top scorer across the whole 2016/17 season?

....

2. Name the two players who joined the Cherries from Liverpool in the 2016/17 season!

....

3. Which club did the Cherries do 'the double' over last season?

....

4. Which goal won the club's Goal of the Season award for the 2016/17?

....

5. How many penalties did Artur Boruc save last season?

....

GOALSCORERS!

These three scored the most Premier League goals for the club last season. But can you guess how many times each player scored? Draw a line from the player to number of goals you think.

JOSHUA KING	7
BENIK AFOBE	16
JUNIOR STANISLAS	6

QUIZ TIME

WHO AM I?

Dan Gosling

WORDSEARCH

```
G S I C N A R F E S G N I M
E A R T E R S L E I N A D P
E B A L E B D A K E B A N U
L B O U A L E D A R G M L G
F K A F N O S L I W H A W H
O H W U A E N I H B G H O L
G W B E G O V I C R A O M E
E S U R M A N R L A D N I W
O G D E C U R O B D T E M I
D R A M S D A L E S I Y E S
D G D A H T I M S M A D A C
E N E B I M A S G I N R N O
M M G O S L I N G T I T B O
N O I E O F E D A H G C H K
```

SHIRTS FROM HISTORY

1999/00 = C	2014/15 = D
2004/06 = B	2015/16 = A
2006/08 = E	

MASSIVE MUDDLE

Asmir Begovic

Connor Mahoney

Charlie Daniels

Tyrone Mings

Jermain Defoe

SQUAD NUMBER CONUNDRUM

1. 12 - Aaron Ramsdale
2. 26 - Tyrone Mings
3. 13 - Callum Wilson
4. 24 - Ryan Fraser

NAUGHTY BOY!

Harry Arter (11)

HEAD TO HEAD!

Adam Smith (5 assists)

NAME THE SIDE

1. Joshua King
2. Artur Boruc
3. Charlie Daniels
4. Junior Stanislas
5. Jack Wilshere
6. Harry Arter
7. Marc Pugh

FIVE QUESTIONS ON

1. Joshua King
2. Brad Smith, Jordon Ibe
3. Swansea City
4. Steve Cook's goal vs Liverpool
5. Two (Crystal Palace, Man Utd)

GOALSCORERS!

Joshua King = 16

Benik Afobe = 6

Junior Stanislas = 7